CONTENTS

Earlene Hilliard

THE

ARM OF

LOVE

*Truths compiled
from the writings of*

FRANCIS
FRANGIPANE

Scripture taken from the New American Standard Bible
© 1960, 1962, 1963, 1968, 1971, 1972, 1973, 1975, 1977
by the Lockman Foundation. Used by permission.

ISBN #1-886296-06-5

1.

SPIRITUAL AUTHORITY AND THE THINGS WE LOVE

While the doctrines of Christianity can be taught, Christlikeness can only be inspired. This next generation of leaders will by their humble and holy lives inspire multitudes. They will truly walk in Christ's love; they will be granted great authority.

Authority to Make Disciples

There are many administrators but few examples of Christ; many teachers but few who walk as Jesus walked. Indeed, while many stand in leadership today, not many function in Christ's authority.

However, a new level of authority is coming to the church. The Holy Spirit is about to crown God's servants with anointed spiritual authority; it will bring healing and deliverance on a scale unprecedented since the first century. In fact, God's promise is that in some cases entire cities will taste salvation.

Spiritual authority is nothing less than God Himself confirming our words with His power. The examples in the Scriptures are plain: Those who are raised up by God are backed up by God. They will **"decree a thing, and it will be established"** (Job 22:28). As He did for Samuel, the Lord will let none of their words fall to the ground, for their words and their authority will be a manifestation of the living God Himself.

Yet, why is there so little true spiritual authority in the church today? The answer lies partly in the fact that the authority of the church has been delegated to it, given only to carry out the purposes of God, and not to accomplish manmade programs and traditions. What are God's purposes? Jesus said, **"All authority has been given to Me in heaven and on earth. Go therefore and make disciples of all the nations"** (Matt 28:18-19).

Christ gave the church authority to make disciples, not merely converts. Many are believers in Jesus, but few are followers of Him. How do we make disciples? Jesus answers that question for us: **"teaching them to observe all that I commanded"** (see Matthew 28:20). When the church returns to teaching all that Jesus taught, our disciples will have authority to do all that Jesus did.

This new level of authority is not something we possess merely because we strive for it. We cannot buy it as Simon the magician attempted to do (see Acts 8:18). The power of authority will not function simply because we copy the methods of another, as the sons of Sceva realized (see Acts 19:14); nor can it be attained automatically because we read books about building the church. We cannot pretend to have spiritual authority. However, there are divinely ordained ways for us to minister in Christ's authority.

Authority to Lay Down Our Lives

From the beginning of our salvation we have enjoyed the Father's unconditional love. As we mature, however, there comes a time when the Father's love toward us seems conditional. As it was for Christ, so it is for those who follow Him. He said, **"For this reason the Father loves Me, because I lay down My life"** (John 10:17). Jesus lived in the deepest intimacies of the Father's love because He laid down His life for the sheep. If we will grow in true authority, we will do so by laying down our lives for His sheep.

Have you felt the drawing, the divine working of the Father, bringing you into Christlike surrender? Be encouraged; He is equipping you for this next outpouring of His Spirit. But also be advised: Your authority will be an outgrowth of your life laid down in love.

Perhaps we have been misled in our understanding of what spiritual authority is and where it comes from. We do not move in true spiritual authority simply because we hold a position in the church. Here is the path to true spiritual authority: The Holy Spirit delivers us from our fears and restores to us the possession of our souls. Then, without being intimidated by the enemy or manipulated by the influence of man, we choose to lay down our lives in obedience to God. Yes, in full freedom, with avenues of escape plainly within our grasp, we fearlessly surrender our souls to the Almighty. No one controls us but God, yet our lives are laid down, like Christ's, for the sins of men.

When we could easily fight and win, yet turn the other cheek; when we are unjustly opposed, yet quietly endure—at those moments spiritual authority is entering our lives.

"No one has taken [My life] **away from Me, but I lay it down on My own initiative"** (John 10:18). Jesus was not forced to accept crucifixion; He *chose* crucifixion. Christ's Gethsemane prayer was not an entreaty to escape the cross, for while Jesus was still in the garden He told Peter, **"Do you think that I cannot appeal to My Father, and He will at once put at My disposal more than twelve legions of angels?"** (Matt 26:53). Jesus had a choice; legions of warring angels and immediate personal deliverance, or death on the cross and deliverance for the world. He chose to die. The willful decision to lay down our lives as Jesus did is the very path upon which true authority develops. Jesus said, **"I have authority to lay** [My life] **down"** (John 10:18). His authority came in the laying down of His life. Our authority comes from the same source: picking up our cross and laying down our lives.

Authority, Not Control

Spiritual authority is the power and provision of God to invade and transform the temporal with the power of the eternal. It is not something our flesh can imitate, nor is it found in the tone of our words or the gaze of our eyes. Divine authority requires divine sanction. This sanction comes from passing the tests of love.

When authority is administered without love, it degenerates into control. God does not call us to control His people, but to inspire and guard them. The outcome of control is oppression, witchcraft, and strife. But the result of love is liberty and the power to build up and protect God's people.

In spiritual authority there is no control involved, nor is any needed. Our lives and the lives of those who follow us are laid down, like Christ's, on our own initiative. It is a choice born out of love. Since true authority itself is born in freedom, freedom is what it breeds.

We will walk in either the true authority of love, the false authority of control, or no authority at all. Both false authority and no authority are rooted in fear, and we react to fear in one of two ways. The first reaction, which produces false authority, is to seek to control those around us, thus making the circumstances around us more predictable and less threatening. The other response to fear is to refuse to accept and exercise any authority at all. Many relationships are simply the pairing of these symbionic needs: the desire to control and the willingness to be controlled. Both are fueled by overreactions to fear.

The Scripture tells us, however, **"There is no fear in love; but perfect love casts out fear"** (1 John 4:18). Since true authority is built upon love, its goal is to liberate, not dominate. Therefore, before one can truly move in spiritual authority he must be delivered from fear and its desire to control; he must be rooted and grounded in love.

Authority to Inspire Christlikeness

When our teaching about God and our obedience to Him are one, spiritual authority accompanies our lives. Jesus astounded the multitudes, for He spoke **"as one having authority"** (Matt 7:29). What He taught was consistent with how He lived. Therefore, we also must live and display the virtue we seek to teach.

If we seek to train our church to pray, we ourselves must first be intercessors. You may say, But out of a congregation of several hundred, only three people join me for prayer. Then those three are the individuals you are truly touching. Do not be discouraged, for you will win others. The measure of our success is not the numbers in attendance Sunday mornings. God has given us people so we may train them, not merely count them. Of this group, those whom we inspire to live like Christ are actually the measure of our success, the test of our effectiveness in the ministry.

You may say, But I've never been a leader. When anyone lays down his or her life in Christ's love, others will see and follow. Such a one can speak with confidence and penetration, whether as a pastor, a housewife, or a child. This next generation will not just teach the people; they will inspire the body of Christ to live like Jesus. Their example in all things will awaken godliness in those around them. From true virtue shall the leaders of tomorrow draw true authority, for when the nature of Christ is revealed, the authority of Christ soon follows.

Authority Born from Love

As wide as our sphere of love is, to that extent we have spiritual authority. We see this in the mother who loves her child. Such a woman has authority to protect, train, and nurture her offspring. She has authority to protect what she loves. The same is true of the husband over his family. His authority is not merely to rule but to establish his home in the life of Christ. True spiritual authority is born of love.

The individuals who love their local church have authority to build up that church. Their authority is not extended, however, beyond the boundaries of their love. If we love the entire body of Christ in a locale, our authority touches the lives of those in our city or region, either through the burden of prayer or through teaching and service.

The testing ground of all spiritual things is love, for love alone purifies our motives and delivers us from the deceitfulness of self. Even authority in warfare must be rooted in love. David gained the skills to slay Goliath by defending his father's sheep from vicious predators; he did not learn these skills on the battlefield. He loved the sheep so much that he would even risk his life for them. So also we grow in authority as we protect our Father's sheep, the flock He has given us to love.

Authority is muscle in the arm of love. The more one loves, the more authority is granted to him. If we love our cities and are willing to lay down our lives for them, God will enlarge our hearts, granting us authority to confront principalities and powers.

However, no man should ever engage in confrontational warfare who does not love what he has been called to protect. If you do not love your city, do not pray against the ruling forces of darkness. Satan knows the genuineness of our love by the brightness of the glory which surrounds us. A man without Christlike love will soon shrink back and fail in spiritual warfare.

Therefore, in His mercy God restrains most Christians from understanding the doctrines of our authority in spiritual warfare. For there are many things He has to say which we are not able to hear until the base of our love is expanded. In His love He protects us from presumptuously attacking the strongholds of hell and suffering loss. Yet if we are truly anointed in God's love, the price to see our cities saved is not too great, for it is the price love always pays: the willingness to die for what we care for.

Authority to Build Up the Body of Christ

"For even if I should boast somewhat further about our authority, which the Lord gave for building you up and not for destroying you, I shall not be put to shame" (2 Cor 10:8).

Many so-called "prophets" today think they are called, like Jeremiah, **"to pluck up and to break down, to destroy and to overthrow"** (Jer 1:10). Jeremiah's message was to a people who were destined to be carried off into Babylon. He spoke to a people who did not have the Holy Spirit and the blood of Jesus, a nation whom God Himself said was destined for captivity (see Jeremiah 12:7).

The whole commission of Jeremiah, though, was more than confronting sin. It also included promises of restoration and deliverance, **"to build and to plant"** (Jer 1:10). To represent the heart of the Lord, which is the true prophetic role, the servant of God must know if the Holy Spirit is preparing to destroy or seeking to rebuild.

Today we are a people coming out of captivity, a people whom God is encouraging to build, as they did in the days of Nehemiah, Ezra, Haggai, and Zechariah. We have been in exile from the promises of God, but we are returning to rebuild the Lord's house. It is not a time to tear down the body of Christ; it is a time to establish and to build up.

The authority coming to the church in this next outpouring will be to restore the local, citywide church. Like Paul's authority, ours will be given for building and encouraging, not for destroying.

God has this new leadership constantly before His eyes. Pastors from many denominations, along with their congregations, are meeting together in prayer, seeking to draw the very fire and heart of God into their souls. Emerging from this foundation of humility and prayer is a new authority to make disciples of Christ. Because their love encompasses the entire city, their authority reaches even into the heavenly places. They are beginning to impact the spiritual atmosphere of their cities; in many cases they are becoming effective against the principalities and powers ruling there. These are the leaders God is raising up, whom He will back up with His power.

Dear Lord, make me a willing sacrifice. I desire Your authority, Lord. Give me courage to surrender in obedience, even when I do not see the outcome and when all I see is loss. Help me to trust as I walk through the narrow gate. Establish in me Your love, that I might defend Your people with authority. In Jesus' name. Amen.

2.

OUR AUTHORITY IN CHRIST

Many saints wonder whether Christians have the authority to pray against principalities and powers. The scriptural position is that we not only have the authority to war against these spiritual enemies, but we have the responsibility to do so! As God leads us, we must pray against them, or they will, indeed, prey upon us.

Our Model is Jesus

In understanding the role and authority of the church in spiritual warfare, we have no other example than Jesus. The Bible tells us that **"we are to grow up in**

all aspects into Him, who is the head, even Christ" (Eph 4:15). The direction of the church is always toward Christlikeness. Thus, only by studying Jesus Himself with a view toward our own personal transformation will the mystery of the church be solved and the purpose of God be accomplished. For the anointing and nature of Christ *are* the call and destiny of the church.

Knowing, therefore, the Father's eternal plan to make man in Christ's image, the Son of God Himself confidently assures us: **"He who believes in Me, the works that I do shall he do also"** (John 14:12). John also connects the nature of Christ with the authority and purpose of the church. He wrote, **"As He is, so also are we in this world"** (1 John 4:17). If we truly desire heaven's endorsement, then our doctrines and objectives must be built upon this one foundation: Truth is in Jesus.

Therefore, let us ask ourselves: Are we doing what Jesus did? For whatever Jesus did, the Spirit-anointed church will do likewise. Did Jesus love? Then those who serve Him will love with His love. Did He pray? Then His disciples will pray with His fervor. And if Christ engaged in spiritual warfare, it follows that His body will also wage war.

Jesus obviously confronted unclean spirits that were resident in the physical and spiritual nature of man. These

Notes

Notes

entities were not simply inherent psycho-
logical weaknesses; they were demons.
Whether it was the Gerasene demoniac
with many demons or the more usual
deliverance of one or two spirits, Jesus
certainly waged spiritual warfare (see
Matthew 8:28-34). And if Jesus cast out
demons, then we should expect His disciples to do likewise, for of His fullness
we have all received (see John 1:16).

Even a casual observer can see that
Jesus had an attitude of war toward Satan.
In fact, all that He did, whether loving,
healing, teaching, or even the simple act
of blessing children, was involved in
destroying the works of Satan.

Jesus also aggressively *pursued* His
enemies. For whenever Jesus perceived
hell's evil workers, He confronted them
in His authority—and He did so without
fear or the slightest hesitation. Even with
the Gerasene demoniac, who was vio-
lently insane and supernaturally power-
ful, Christ fearlessly and immediately
engaged Himself in warfare with the
man's tormentors.

Furthermore, knowing the ongoing
state of war which would exist after
He left, we see Jesus building a church
to prevail against the gates of hell. Jesus
sent forth His disciples, instructing them
to cast out demons and giving them
**"authority . . . over all the power of the
enemy"** (Luke 10:19; see also Matthew
16:19; Luke 9:1).

18

Remember, our model is none other than Jesus. Not only did He live without fear, but demons were terrified of Him! He was never presumptuous, yet just His gaze flooded evil spirits with trembling and torment. Consider: Christ's promise to everyone who believes in Him is that **"greater works than these shall [you] do; because I go to the Father"** (John 14:12).

Christ and Principalities and Powers

The question arises, But did Jesus confront principalities and powers? We have no gospel account of His challenging the ruling powers over Israel. In fact, we find no mention of the word "principality" in any of Christ's discourses. However, He is apparently speaking with reference to both principalities and powers in Matthew 24:29, where He states that before He returns **"the powers of the heavens will be shaken."**

Although we do not find scriptural examples of His addressing evil powers as such, the above question might be better rephrased to ask: Did Jesus confront the kingdom of darkness on any level higher than demonic possession? Yes, Jesus clashed with the prince of darkness, Satan himself.

Christ's war was even beyond the territorial battle associated with principalities and powers. Although regionally located, His spiritual warfare was global in consequence. He did not come merely to redeem a city or a nation but the world. The fact is that, when the Prince of Peace came, the prince of darkness rose to meet Him: Satan was Jesus' adversary.

New Levels, New Devils

As I see it, there is a type of order to spiritual warfare. Satan himself does not attack new Christians, nor does the Lord require new Christians to attack the type of principalities or powers that rule over nations and certain ethnic and religious groups. Satan, the former archangel, does not have to personally attack Christians when a minor demon can sidetrack most of us.

Contrary to what we may think, Lucifer, as he was formerly called, rarely attacks individuals. In my opinion, there are probably fewer than forty individuals in today's world who are actually considered a threat and worthy of his focused, steadfast attention. It would be safe to say that most spiritual warfare is an exercise in authority over demons. Few Christians will be called to confront the highest level of principalities and powers.

Evil spirits are assigned against us proportionately, according to the threat we may pose to hell. With each new spiritual level attained, there is a fiercer, more adept enemy awaiting us. And while only some might actually face Satan himself, many in the church today are being trained and anointed to mobilize the church and defeat the ruling evil spirits in their regions.

In the first century, Christ's apostles were of such a stature that they actually became a threat not only to principalities and powers, but to the devil himself. In response to their personal confrontations with Satan, they unhesitatingly wrote their warnings in the Scriptures and also gave instructions on how to overcome.

It should be noted that, when the Scriptures speak specifically about the devil, the usual inference is that the writer is referring to the more typical battle against an evil spirit and not the devil himself. The precepts they applied against Satan work with every level of demonic attack, whether a principality or power, a demon or an imp.

From his own confrontations with Satan, for example, Peter speaks of the devil as a **"roaring lion, seeking someone to devour."** Yet he said to remain **"firm in your faith,"** and God will supply the power to **"resist"** him (see 1 Peter 5:8-9). James also speaks of spiritual warfare. From his experience with spiritual attacks he writes, **"Submit therefore to God. Resist the devil and he will flee from you"** (James 4:7). You, as a new creation in Christ, have the power to resist the devil. Out of your submission to Christ, Satan will actually flee from you!

In speaking to the young men in the church, the apostle John wrote, **"You are**

Notes

strong, and the word of God abides in you, and you have overcome the evil one" (1 John 2:14). He reminds us that Jesus came to "destroy the works of the devil" (1 John 3:8). John goes so far as to say that "greater is He who is in [us] than he who is in the world" (1 John 4:4) and that there is a place of hiddenness in Christ where the evil one cannot touch us at all.

The Church at God's Throne

So we see that Jesus exercised authority over all the power of the enemy and that He gave this same authority to the church. It is our task to follow Him. Every pastor needs to know when a situation calls for counseling and encouragement or when a demonic stronghold must be confronted and spiritual authority exercised. For more information on this subject we suggest reading *The Three Battlegrounds* by this author.

Because of the increasing battle at the end of this age, each one of us should know the scriptural basis of our authority in Christ. Paul wrote,

I pray that the eyes of your heart may be enlightened, so that you may know what is the hope of His calling, what are the riches of the glory of His inheritance in the saints, and what is the surpassing greatness of His power toward us who believe (Eph 1:18-19).

Through your faith in God there is a divine power being directed toward you even now as you read this. Paul says this power is *the very same power* which resurrected Jesus,

> **which He brought about in Christ, when He raised Him from the dead, and seated Him at His right hand in the heavenly places, far above all rule and authority and power and dominion** (Eph 1:20-21).

All true Christians believe Jesus Christ is Lord and that He is seated at the right hand of God. Theologically we are in agreement about Christ's positional authority. What we fail to see is *our* authority as Christ's body and His agents upon earth. Paul continues,

> **And He put all things in subjection under His feet, and gave Him as head over all things to the church, which is His body, the fulness of Him who fills all in all** (Eph 1:22-23).

Notice three key words: *feet, head,* and *body*. Jesus is head of a body which has feet; under His feet all things have been put in subjection. The Holy Spirit is not limiting the subjection of all things to be under Christ's physical feet at the throne of God. No! The context is plain: Christ is head over a *body* (see 1 Corinthians 12:12); all things are under the *feet* of that body. The "feet" are those members which walk upon the earth.

The feet do not have one authority and the head another; rather, as long as the feet are in subjection to the head and carrying out His will, their authority *is* the expansion of His authority. Notice also that the **"things in subjection"** include by name principalities and powers. Note also that this phrase **"in subjection"** is a military term, speaking of the victor's authority over the vanquished.

Paul is stating here that through the yielded, obedient church the authority of Jesus is exhibited in militant and triumphant victory over all the power of the devil, even over principalities and powers in the heavenly places. No wonder Paul began this discourse by saying, **"I pray that the eyes of your heart may be enlightened"** (Eph 1:18).

The typical self-concept of church members is earthly in nature. However, Paul tells us that there is another dimension to "new creation" people. He says that God **"raised us up with Him, and seated us with Him in the heavenly places, in Christ Jesus"** (Eph 2:6). Jesus does not have one seat next to the Father and another seat next to us in the heavenly places. The **"heavenly places"** seat and God's **"right hand"** seat are the same place. He has raised us up and seated us with Him far above all rule and authority and power and dominion.

Right now, spiritually and positionally, through the redemptive life of Christ, we are part of an army which is at the same time both earthly and heavenly in nature. The fact is, if Christ is truly with us here, then we are indeed with Him there. For Christ and His church are one.

The Father's Promise to His Son

Psalm 110:1 documents a most amazing conversation. We discover in this text a promise spoken by the Father directly to His Son. It reads, **"The Lord says to my Lord: 'Sit at My right hand, until I make Thine enemies a footstool for Thy feet.' "** God the Father is set upon making Christ's enemies a footstool for His feet. We are not learning about warfare because we, on our own initiative, decided to learn it. God Himself has chosen to equip us to fulfill His promise to His Son.

In effect the Father said to His Son, "I resurrected You, bringing You through all eternity to seat You next to Me on My throne. Rest at My right hand. The Holy Spirit will unite You with those who believe. Spiritually, they will actually become Your body; those living on the earth will become as Your feet. As the God of peace, I will crush Satan beneath Your 'feet' " (see Romans 16:20).

Psalm 110 is the Old Testament passage that supported Paul's revelation to the Ephesians. The very same power God used to raise Jesus is now training us to tread upon serpents and scorpions, and it is giving us authority over all the power of the enemy (see Luke 10:19). We have

been granted this authority as a fulfillment of the promise between the Father
and His Son.

The Voice of God

We must learn to use the authority of
Christ, not presumptuously, but adminis-
tratively and compassionately. For there
is an unparalleled spiritual assault against
cities and our children by the enemy. Yet
the weapons of our warfare are mighty.
Additionally, the Lord Himself is shaking the powers of darkness in the heavenly places.

**"On that day the Lord will punish
the fallen angels in the heavens, and the
proud rulers of the nations on earth"**
(Isa 24:21 LB). While we are seeing with
our own eyes the beginnings of the Lord's
punishment of the proud rulers of the
nations, especially in the communist
countries, we do not see the Lord's punishment of the **"fallen angels in the
heavens."** He is toppling the principalities and powers whose influence seemed
unshakable.

The Lord has promised a shaking at
the end of the age that will topple all
things. We read in Hebrews that **"He has
promised, saying, 'Yet once more I will
shake not only the earth, but also the
heaven' "** (Heb 12:26).

The **"heaven"** to which this text
refers is the heavenly places, the spiritual
realm which immediately surrounds the
earth. This text tells us that prior to His

return, the Lord will speak a word which will shake and cleanse even the spirit realm surrounding our world. Hebrews continues,

> **This expression, "Yet once more," denotes the removing of those things which can be shaken, as of created things, in order that those things which cannot be shaken may remain. Therefore, since we receive a kingdom which cannot be shaken, let us show gratitude** (Heb 12:27-28).

God is going to remove the proud rulers of the earth and the demonic rulers from the heavenlies. He is doing it right before our eyes. As the wrestling continues between the church and the hosts of hell, we are beginning to learn the enemy's moves.

We know how to submit to God and resist the devil, and we can discern the "accuser of the brethren." We have learned to anticipate and protect ourselves against temptation, to stand in spite of fear, and to persevere even while we are weary. And knowing that every demon is a liar, we know not to listen to or believe the voice of our adversary.

We also are learning the Lord's "moves." We know Christ's humility is our armor, His love is our strength, and His forgiveness disarms demons. We know the power of the blood, the authority of Jesus' name, and the importance of

Notes

our testimony. We are no longer ignorant of Satan's devices. We know it is our eternal destiny to win this war!

God has something to say to the "authorities in the heavenly places." And it is the wisdom of God that *the church,* the once-fallen but now cleansed and redeemed church, should be His vehicle to complete His judgment of the devil.

For those who question the timing of all this, Paul tells us that this ministry of God is not just **"in the [age] to come"** (Eph 1:21), but **"now . . . through the church to the rulers and the authorities"** (Eph 3:10). The first-century church was an instrument of God unto principalities and powers. So also will the last earthly church be used by God in spiritual warfare.

3.

THE TWO SIDES OF GOD'S TRUTH

During the past few years there has been an ongoing debate concerning the doctrine of "strategic level spiritual warfare." The controversy orbits around a single question: *Do Christians have authority to confront the powers of darkness?*

Those who say "yes" can support their view with a number of scriptures (see Luke 10:19; Ephesians 1:18-23; 6:10-17, etc.), while those who say "no" base much of their perspective on the lack of biblical examples of high level warfare, especially in the book of Acts. Both positions are espoused by respected teachers. While they currently seem to be at odds with each other, if we listen humbly, we may find God's heart is revealed in both.

Knowing God's Ways

All of us agree that "spiritual warfare" should never be approached casually. A great disservice has been done by some who, seeing spiritual warfare as the latest trend, flippantly enter into battle. Because of immaturity, they often end up inflicting more wounds on themselves and others than on the enemy.

Any authority God gives us in spiritual warfare should never be empowered by zeal or human initiative. It is delegated by God to carry out His strategies in His timing. Much of the ineffectiveness that occurs today is simply because we are running ahead of the Lord. We must seek His discernment to know what God is fighting against *now*.

Clearly, the church in America is in a time of *training* and *preparation*. We still argue too much among ourselves; we are still a house divided. We cannot effectively stand before our enemy if we have not first knelt together before God.

God's purpose with the church is to make us a dwelling for Christ. Our spiritual assault against the enemy actually begins in our personal consecration to God. Jesus Christ must be functionally revealed in our behavior, our words, and our love toward others. Only as He manifests in us on earth are we manifested with Him in spiritual warfare in the heavenlies. *It is His presence within us which secures both our safety and authority in battle.*

Our singular weapon against principalities and powers is **"the sword of the Spirit, which is the word of God"** (Eph 6:17). We *must* know what God is saying, for the armies in heaven follow Him—**"and His name is called The Word of God"** (Rev 19:13). Our victory comes from following, proclaiming, and obeying the Word of God.

If we, for example, presumptuously command "mammon" to fall, but it is not a word spoken and confirmed by God, the first place mammon is likely to fall is on us. You see, it must be Christ who fills us and speaks through us in His anointing.

That Which is Born of the Spirit

Many who dispute "strategic level warfare" argue that only angels, or Christ Himself, can exercise authority over regional or national principalities and powers. They feel that the church, being physical, has authority only in the physical world; we are outside our domain when we pray directly against the devil. In short, only if the enemy manifests in the physical world do they feel we have any authority over him.

The logic in this approach is that one's spiritual "level" defines the range of his authority: angels for the spiritual world and man for the natural realm world. We agree with the concept that our spiritual "level" defines our authority. But we refute the position that the nature of church is merely physical.

A Christian is not just flesh and blood, nor is our spiritual place of abiding limited to the physical universe. Although Paul was a man, he exercised authority beyond the physical realm. He said,

> **For, although we are in the flesh, we do not battle according to the flesh, for the weapons of our battle are not of flesh but are enormously powerful, capable of destroying fortresses** (2 Cor 10:3-4 NAB).

The Lord Jesus said, **"That which is born of the flesh is flesh, and that which is born of the Spirit is spirit"** (John 3:6). If we are truly born again, then we are a new creation, a hybrid consisting of both a flesh nature *and* a spirit nature. The Lord told Nicodemus, **"Do not marvel that I said to you, 'You must be born again [*from above*, Ampl]' "** (John 3:7). We should not judge Nicodemus too harshly for his spiritual dullness. We all struggle with accepting our spiritual identity.

Scripture tells us that the church is **"seated . . . with [Christ] in the heavenly places"** (Eph 2:6). Although we physically dwell on earth, spiritually we are positioned in Christ, **"far above all rule and authority and power and dominion, and every name that is named . . . in this age [and] in the one to come"** (Eph 1:21). We have a scriptural platform to stand "level to level" against principalities and powers.

Because we have a spirit-based nature, and are not just physical, we have a dual role in the administration of God's authority. We are called to defend our world from both spiritual and natural forces of evil. The positional authority level of the church in this age spans both the physical and spiritual realms.

Of course, we do not have the same *conscious awareness* as angels; we walk by faith, not sight. Certainly our relationship to principalities and powers is limited to how these spirits interact with mankind. We have no authority beyond this. And, it will be an angel, not a man, which ultimately binds up the devil for 1,000 years.

Yet, while our authority is limited to this extent, under Christ's direction, the spiritual authority of His Church can be quite effective in the world today.

An Example

Over the last few years at River of Life, the Lord has spoken to our hearts that He wanted us to join Him in His war against the accuser of the brethren. What was the first phase of His strategy? He showed us that we had no authority over

Notes

anything outside of us, if we were compromising with it inside of us. During a period of several months He continued a process of delivering us from faultfinding and accusation amongst ourselves, calling us to walk as He walked in redemptive intercession.

As the Lord began cleansing us within, He also began increasing His anointing for battle, giving us initiatives within specific *limitations*. He instructed us to fight the accuser's influence primarily *in the church, not* over cities. Judgment begins first with the household of God. His justice forbids judging the world, which is ignorant of His ways, if the church itself has not modeled righteousness.

He has made us aware that the enemy occupies strongholds in the church. We found that before we could successfully deal with the accuser, we also had to deal with the sympathetic thoughts in the church toward accusation. So, we began teaching against faultfinding and accusation, bringing our leadership to repentance and then our church.

Utilizing our publications, and also through conferences and the media, we are now pursuing this enemy on a larger scale. Because the Lord has gone before us in this, by conservative estimates over 15 million believers have heard this message. In nearly 400 cities, thousands of churches from various backgrounds are putting away their differences and are, in increasing measures, returning to Jesus in prayer.

Our approach has been to bind the strongman before we can distribute his goods. But Jesus said we must also take away the armor upon which he relied (Luke 11:21-22). Satan's armor is our unrepentant thought life. We cannot defeat him if he is sheltered in the carnal thoughts of God's people.

Thus, Paul sought to bring the Corinthians into Christ's likeness, where the corporate church learned to take **"every thought captive to the obedience of Christ"** (2 Cor 10:5). Then, with the highest purposes of God satisfied, the anointing for warfare follows.

Better Things for Us

Why is the book of Acts silent concerning strategic level warfare? One possible answer is that it was not yet God's timing. Scripture indicates that it will not be until the end of the age, just before Christ returns, that the "powers of the heavens" are shaken (see Matthew 24:29).

It is also within the pattern of the Scriptures that God's promise to one generation is inherited by another (see Hebrews 11:39-40; 1 Peter 1:10-12). There are *many* promises the first century saints knew only in part that we shall possess in fulfillment. For the glory of the latter house shall be greater than the former.

Notes

Yet, Paul wrote as a man who knew he had God's strategy. Just as he anticipated resurrection and wrote of it in Philippians 3:10, so he wrote in faith concerning confrontational warfare. Yet it remains a promise to be fulfilled in God's time. Paul modeled his stance against principalities and powers in Ephesians 6:12-18. And to the Corinthians, he stood **"ready to punish all disobedience, whenever [their] obedience is complete"** (2 Cor 10:6).

DISCIPLESHIP TRAINING BOOKLETS
2.50 each (10 or more at 40%, 100 or more at 50% discount)

COMPILED/FORMATTED FOR GROUP STUDY BY FRANCIS FRANGIPANE

LOVE & DEVOTION SERIES:

A Time to Seek God

CHAPTERS: THE TENT OF MEETING; TWO THINGS, TWO THINGS ONLY; UNRELENTING LOVE; DRAWING NEAR TO THE HOLY GOD; A PLACE FOR HIM TO REST; THE WAY INTO THE HOLY PLACE ISBN 1-886296-00-6 #FF1-020

The Baptism of Love

CHAPTERS: BEWARE OF COLD LOVE; LOVE: GOD'S PRESERVATIVE; THE BAPTISM OF LOVE; FORGIVENESS AND THE FUTURE OF YOUR CITY
ISBN 1-886296-09-X #FF1-016

SPIRITUAL AUTHORITY & PRAYER SERIES:

Prevailing Prayer

CHAPTERS: LEGAL PROTECTION; DAY AND NIGHT PRAYER; SENT BY GOD; REPENTANCE PRECEDES REVIVAL; COVENANT POWER
ISBN 1-886296-01-4 #FF1-011

The Arm of Love

CHAPTERS: OUR AUTHORITY IN CHRIST; SPIRITUAL AUTHORITY AND THE THINGS WE LOVE; THE TWO SIDES OF GOD'S TRUTH
ISBN 1-886296-06-5 #FF1-015

CHURCH UNITY SERIES:

Repairers of the Breach

CHAPTERS: THE SON'S ANSWERED PRAYER; REPAIRERS OF THE BREACH; WHEN THE LORD BUILDS HIS HOUSE
ISBN 1-886296-05-7 #FF1-013

By Wisdom the House is Built

CHAPTERS: BY WISDOM THE HOUSE IS BUILT; THE ANOINTING TO BUILD; IT TAKES A CITY-WIDE CHURCH; THE STONE WHICH BUILDERS REJECTED   ISBN 1-886296-07-3 #FF1-014

DISCERNMENT SERIES:

Exposing the Accuser of the Brethren

CHAPTERS: EXPOSING THE ACCUSER; CASTING DOWN THE ACCUSER; PROTECTED FROM THE ACCUSER; AT THE THRONE WITH GOD
ISBN 0-9629049-6-1 #FF1-017

A bestseller on how to protect yourself and prosper in the midst of battle.

Discerning of Spirits

CHAPTERS: THE GIFT OF DISCERNMENT; ELIMINATING FALSE DISCERNMENT; DISCERNING THE NATURE OF THE ENEMY; THE STRONGHOLD OF CHRIST'S LIKENESS.
ISBN 0-9629049-7-X #FF1-018

The Jezebel Spirit

CHAPTERS: DISCERNING THE SPIRIT OF JEZEBEL; ELIJAH, JEHU AND THE WAR AGAINST JEZEBEL; OUR EXPERIENCE WITH JEZEBEL; STRATEGY AGAINST THE SPIRIT OF JEZEBEL; FREE TO LAUGH   ISBN 0-9629049-8-8 #FF1-019

Exposing Witchcraft

CHAPTERS: KEYS UNLOCK GATES; EXPOSING WITCHCRAFT!; HOW WITCHCRAFT WORKS; GOD'S GREAT MERCY; SYMPTOMS OF WITCHCRAFT; "WITCHCRAFT" IN THE CHURCH; GOD'S SHELTER AGAINST WITCHCRAFT; BRINGING A SATANIST TO CHRIST; "OH, WHAT GOD HAS DONE!"
ISBN 1-886296-02-2 #FF1-012

Booklets by Denise Frangipane

DELIVERANCE FROM PMS

PRACTICAL AND SPIRITUAL HELPS TOWARD DELIVERANCE FROM PMS. ISBN 1-886296-03-0 #DF1-002

OVERCOMING FEAR!

TESTIMONY & KEYS TO RELEASING THE POWER OF FAITH.   ISBN 1-886296-04-9 #DF1-003